A Page *Of* Hope

A Self Help Guide for Delinquent Homeowners

By

MELISSA SOLIS

IMPORTANT NOTICE: The information in this book is not intended to serve as legal advice, and should be used at your own risk. Any information and third party referrals may change or be updated.

Limit of Liability/Disclaimer of Warranty: While the author has used the best efforts in preparing this book, they make no representation or warranties with respect to the accuracy or completeness of the contents and specifically disclaim any implied warranties. This book is for informational purposes only and the author does not accept any responsibilities for any liabilities resulting from the use of this information. The author and referrals cannot assume any responsibilities for errors, inaccuracies or omissions. All names and dates have been changed to protect identities.

Copyright

© 2013 Melissa Solis. This book is protected under the US Copyright law and other applicable federal state and local laws. All rights are reserved. No part of this book may be reproduced or transmitted, in any form or by any means, electronic, mechanical, photocopying, recording or otherwise without prior permission.

CONTENTS

Third Party Companies: Watch out for Copy Cats 5
Is it a waste of bureaucracy? 9
Third Party Authorization 11
Making Home Affordable Plan 12
In-House Options 25
Lack of communication 34
Asking for a loan modification 36
Common Loan Modifications 38
Common Misconceptions about the MHA Program 40
Additional Properties 42
Our Cultural Beliefs 43
Collections Department 44
Hardship Documentation 45
Resubmitting Documentation 48
Getting the Runaround 53
Making a Complaint against your Mortgage Servicer 55
Importance of Contacting the Mortgage Servicer 58
Dealing with Being Denied 58
Credit Report 60

CONTENTS

Contracts/Forms/Deadlines   61
Children Affected By Foreclosures 62
During An Active Foreclosure 64
Filing Bankruptcy   66
Short Sale   67
Getting Treated For a Nervous Breakdown   70
Transitioning From Home 73
Temporary Housing 75
Struggling Homeowners   76
Referrals 100

"Be kind, for everyone you meet is fighting a hard battle."
–Plato

Acknowledgements

First and foremost I would like to thank *God*. I am a woman of God. I am thankful and grateful for the strength and passion He has instilled in me to write.

Homeowners, you are the main reason I put this together. You trusted in me and expressed to me your personal life. Thank you for being honest and sharing your side of the story.

To my fiancé, Chad W. and my daughter, Christa W. I am so thankful I have you in my corner pushing me. Thank you for believing in me and knowing that I could do this. I love you always and forever.

To Veronica Nunez, thank you for assisting me in the process. You are a great mentor.

Many of you don't know what happens behind closed doors. Some of us have lost our jobs or our homes, and in turn, have lost our faith.

Celebrities, government officials, and the average consumer have been foreclosed. Who is responsible when you get the runaround from the mortgage company? Foreclosure is a fungus, a virus spreading widely. Losing your home may cause a loss of family members, friends, or even peace of mind. Losing your home may lead to depression or anxiety. In a worst-case scenario, it can affect a homeowner's health and even lead to death.

Therefore, what do you do when you are in denial and cannot imagine the possibility of losing your home that you once worked so hard for?
It's an ongoing situation.

Homeowners have been trying to receive assistance for the past three years. Regardless of what the servicer says, at the end of the day, homes are foreclosed. A few homeowners are fortunate enough to be awarded with assistance, but many others are not.

The majority of homeowners want their loans to be modified. Homeowners are under the impression that HUD counselors will negotiate a loan modification. However, certified HUD counselors are unable to guarantee your modification. Final decisions are determined by the investor of your loan. However, counselors can educate homeowners, on their loss mitigation options and how to prevent a foreclosure.

Housing counseling sessions are educational. The HUD counselor will review your overall financial situation and make recommendations. HUD counselors will guide you based on your overall situation.

It's impossible for many homeowners to stay abreast of the housing industry, because they have limited time.

"We are too busy seeking employment; it's impossible to keep up with the housing industry."-Homeowner.

Some homeowners have suggested that the government isn't assisting enough. I have come across several homeowners that are under the impression that the government program is a "law." The **Making Home Affordable plan is not a law,** it is a government program, just like food stamps, or Medicaid/Medicare.

I can't speak for every homeowner because every homeowner has a different type of hardship. Whether it's a death in the family, loss of income, or loss of employment, they want immediate assistance.

Homeowners cry, yell, and get confused, because they are bombarded with so much information. They get upset with HUD counselors, bank associates, and loan officers when they are denied for loan modifications. Is it all worth it? This is a crisis, not just an educational course.

As an experienced HUD counselor, I know it may become overwhelming for the consumer to review all the housing programs and options all at once. It takes time and education to have a clear view of what government programs and options are being offered as well as which options they may qualify for.

We want someone to quickly answer us and sometimes we get the run around. It doesn't take one specific website or answer to find out if a homeowner qualifies. It takes hours of education to understand how programs and options work. The following chapters include steps, advice, questions, and referrals that may guide you as a homeowner, before or during delinquency.

Third Party Companies:

Watch out for Copy Cats!

Be careful! If you come across a third party agency that requires a payment for a loan modification, most likely it's a scam. There are third party agencies known as "copy cats." They advertise loan modifications. In fact, they guarantee you a modification on the spot, which is what makes them sound so enticing and is part of their persuasion tactics. However, that's impossible, because servicers require specific documentation to be reviewed by a loan processor and underwriter, which takes weeks to determine qualification.

So how do these copy cats get your information? Most of your information is public record. Copy cats may find out if your home is delinquent or in the foreclosure process. Before sharing any personal information over the phone, confirm with your servicer if they called. Copy cats may also request your bank account information and/or for you to sign documentation. To find out if the third party is legitimate company, contact your state attorney general, U.S. Department of Housing (HUD), or the Better Business Bureau.

Third party housing counseling agencies do not charge. They provide numerous services along with educating homeowners on how to avoid a foreclosure. Due to legal reasons, HUD certified counselors are unable to complete the hardship application for you, or advise you how to fill it out. They can however, provide useful information about the package and additional documents the servicer may request.

It is also recommended to contact the servicer directly if you have questions in regard to the application.

If you contact a third party agency verify it is certified by U.S. Department of Housing. A nonprofit housing agency is an agency paid by nonprofit organizations and/or government agencies. Certified housing counselors educate homeowners about the housing industry. Their goal is to educate you. There is a misconception that they will modify your loan. Their goal is to educate you about the housing industry as well as any and all options available. For example, if you need to make a decision regarding your delinquent mortgage or home purchase, they make recommendations based on your overall situation.

Housing counselors are trained on recent housing programs, options, and grant information. However, they are unable to guarantee your outcome. The outcome will be based on your investor's guidelines. Your lender/servicer reviews your investor's guidelines to determine your eligibility. Your investor has very specific guidelines your servicer has to follow. The Servicer reviews the current hardship, type of hardship, rules, and regulations of the investor to determine if the borrower is eligible.

Is it a waste of bureaucracy?

Homeowners believe mortgage companies use a blockage mechanism to force a homeowner into a foreclosure. Some homeowners believe housing counseling services are a waste of time and may seek assistance on their own. Several homeowners are disappointed with how advertising leads them to believe third party agencies make the final decision, when in reality it is the underwriter of their loan who decides; based on the investor's guidelines. Housing counselors are unable to guarantee the final outcome.

As a result, housing counseling is not intended for every homeowner. Some homeowners might feel they can accomplish the process on their own.

However, servicers might require the completion of a housing counseling session when applying for hardship assistance.

Third Party Authorization

If you are frustrated from speaking to the lender, seek mortgage counseling. In order to have a third party speak to your servicer, your servicer will require either a verbal or written authorization.

If a conference call is initiated, your servicer will want to verify your personal information and will document the third party information. Housing counselors or realtors may then speak on behalf of your loan and ask questions to find out if you are eligible for any assistance.

Regardless of who is assisting you, communication is imperative. Speaking to your servicer is extremely important. If you need assistance with a conference call, contact a non-profit counseling agency.

Making Home Affordable Plan

The following is a brief description of the Making Home Affordable Plan (MHA), a government program. The options are to either keep the home or sell the home or deed in lieu. Each option is based on your investor's guidelines. The ultimate goal is to avoid foreclosure.

Making Home Affordable is a program, not a law. In 2009, the Treasury Department launched the MHA Program. In 2013 Obama extended the application deadline to December 31, 2015.

For program descriptions and pre-approved guidelines, please contact a HUD-approved counselor and visit **www.makinghomeaffordable.gov**. Also, verify if your investor and Mortgage Company are participating in the program.

If your investor is participating in the MHA program, it is in their best interest to review you for the MHA program. A homeowner and lender/servicer may be eligible for an incentive after demonstrating they have been current on their mortgage for five years.

Keep in mind, however, that investors are not obligated to participate in any government programs. Government programs have a number of investors that have chosen to participate. Find out if your investor is participating by contacting the lender directly. If your investor is not participating in the MHA program, ask your servicer what other options are available. At times, the investor (owner of your mortgage loan) may implement traditional, in-house options or programs.

1. Making Home Affordable Refinance known as ***HARP***

2. FHA Short Refinance known as ***FHA SHORT REFI***

3. Making Home Affordable Modification known as ***HAMP***

4. FHA Home Affordable Modification Program known as ***FHA HAMP***

5. Veteran's Affairs Home Affordable Modification known as ***VA HAMP***

6. Second Lien Modification known as ***2MP***

7. Second Lien Modification Program for FHA known as ***FHA 2 LP***

8. Making Home Affordable Unemployment Program known as ***UP***

9. Making Home Affordable Principle Reduction known as ***PRA***

10. Making Home Affordable Short Sale or Deed in Lieu known as ***HAFA***

11. Hardest Hit Fund known as ***HHF***

12. USDA's Special Loan Servicing

Refinance (HARP)

HARP is for homeowners who are current, less than 30 days delinquent, or are unable to refinance due to home not having enough value.

1. Investor of your loan must be Fannie Mae or Freddie Mac. Fannie Mae at 800.732.6643. Freddie Mac at 800.373.3443

2. You may contact any other lender that is participating with HARP.

3. There might be closing costs involved.

4. Expires December 31, 2015.

5. Loan to Value/Debt Ratio will have to be reviewed to make a determination.

Contact your servicer/lender for updated pre-eligibly criteria. Also visit **www.makinghomeaffordable.gov** for the latest updates.

Loan Modification (HAMP)

HAMP may either lower the interest rate, or extend the years on the loan.

GSE, Fannie Mae, Freddie Mac are encouraged to participate.

1. HAMP does not require a homeowner to be delinquent.

2. Obtained home before January 1, 2009.

3. Servicer is not obligated to participate.

4. Homeowner needs proof of hardship and proof to support a modified payment.

5. May require the homeowner to make (3) trial payments.

6. HAMP expires December 31, 2015.

7. If homeowner remains current on the HAMP program for five years they may be awarded $1000, each year,

for up to five years (totaling $5000). The incentive will be applied towards the principle balance of their loan.

HAMP may be updated occasionally, therefore it is important to contact the servicer and visit www.makinghomeaffordable.gov for the latest update.

Trial payments

MHA trial payments were initially implemented for three months. However, there have been cases where a trial payment program may be extended more than three months. If a homeowner is on an MHA trial payment for more than three months they must keep a record of the agreement.

Key points to remember:

1. An MHA trial payment is a temporary payment arrangement.

2. Trial payments are reported to the credit bureau.

3. A trial payment does not guarantee a HAMP.

Second lien Modification (2MP)

Lowers payment on a second lien with specific guidelines. Servicer is not obligated to participate in the (2MP) Second Lien Modification Program.

1. First mortgage may be required to have been modified through the HAMP program.

2. Must not have missed more than three payments on the (first lien) modified loan.

3. Program expires December 31, 2015.

Unemployment Program (UP)

Unemployment program is considered temporary assistance for those who are unemployed.

1. Homeowner must be eligible for unemployment benefits and need to prove they have been receiving benefits for three months.
2. Mortgage payment must be more than 31% of the gross income but criteria may be waived.
3. Have not received HAMP.
4. Loan has to be originated on or before January 1, 2009.

Principle Reduction Alternative (PRA)

PRA is a principle reduction relief program for homes that have had a loss of value and owe more than what the home is worth.

1. This is after the loan is modified through MHA HAMP Program.
2. This is an optional program offered. Verify with servicer to determine if your investor is participating.
3. Must not be owned by Fannie Mae or Freddie Mac.
4. Mortgage payment is more than 31% of gross monthly income.
5. Mortgage obtained on or before January 1, 2009
6. Program expires December 31, 2015.

Short Sale or Deed in Lieu (HAFA)

HAFA Program is for homeowners who can no longer afford the home and decide to sell the home, in order to avoid the foreclosure. Each investor will have specific criteria/guidelines.

1. Short Sale: Selling home for less than what you owe.

2. Deed in lieu: Returning the home to lender after an effort of trying to sell.

3. Some programs may provide an incentive to assist with relocation.

In-House Options

If your servicer does not participate with the Making Home Affordable program, ask for in-house options, or traditional mortgage options. As I mentioned earlier, all options have specific guidelines based on your investor. The following are examples of in-house options.

Refinance

Refinancing programs are recommended for homeowners who are either in imminent default or current.

1. Homeowner is less than 30 days delinquent.
2. It may not always lower your mortgage payment.
3. Interest rate may be reduced.
4. Closing costs might be involved.
5. Your credit score, financials, and home value will determine eligibility.

Reverse Mortgage

1. A reverse mortgage is a mortgage loan based on the equity. This will allow the homeowner to bring the mortgage current.
2. Must live in the home.
3. Own your home or have a low balance.
4. Must be 62 years and older.
5. No monthly principal or interest payments.
6. Must be a single family home or HUD-approved manufactured home or condominium.

For more information visit **http://hud.gov** or contact the *National Council on Aging* at (800) 510-0301.

Repayment Plan

1. The past due amount is divided into either several months or years until the mortgage is brought current.

2. Mortgage payment may increase.

3. Servicer may require a down payment.

Forbearance

1. It may either reduce or suspend your mortgage payment for a short-term period.
2. Homeowner must be less than 12 months delinquent.
3. Once forbearance is complete, the monthly amount suspended or reduced will either be divided into the monthly mortgage payment or added to the principle balance.
(Verify with the terms of the plan)

Loan Modification

Restructuring the loan, modifying any of the terms.

1. Homeowner may be current or in default.
2. If loan is modified the interest rate may change.
3. Years on the loan may be extended. For example, a 30-year loan extended into a 40-year loan.
4. Past due amount might be added towards the end of balance.
5. There are long-term and short-term modifications.
6. Loan must be modified directly with servicer.

Partial Claim (FHA)

1. Partial claim is for homeowners that have an FHA loan.
2. It is an interest free loan to pay past due amount.
3. Homeowner should have stable income.
4. Homeowner should be less than 12 months delinquent.

Short Sale

Short Sale: Selling the home for less than what you owe. If the home has lost value, the servicer will allow the homeowner to sell the home for less than the balance.

1. Seek an experienced short sale realtor.
2. Homeowner should ask servicer if the difference/balance will be forgiven.
3. Investor might offer an incentive to transition from the home.

Deed in Lieu

Returning the (deed) home to servicer as a written agreement.

1. Avoids foreclosure and has less of an effect on the credit score.
2. Certain servicers might offer an incentive to transition from the home.
3. Apply ahead of time, as deed in lieu is a time-consuming process.

Lenders and servicers have specific departments that handle specific loss mitigation options and/or government programs. If there is a change in circumstances, I encourage you to reapply. Call each week for updates; be persistent, as investors' guidelines may change/update.

Lack of communication

The following scenario is a borrower who was foreclosed due to lack of communication.

For more than six months, the borrower had been working with a realtor on a short sale. The homeowner was under the assumption that the realtor kept all lines of communication open with the servicer. The realtor and borrower submitted the requested short sale documentation to the servicer. The realtor called the servicer sporadically.

The realtor indicated he had not heard from the mortgage company. The realtor was under the assumption the homeowner had spoken to the mortgage company. After submitting the documentation, the realtor and homeowner did not follow up with the servicer. The servicer ended up closing the case due to missing documentation.

All parties avoided communication.

Regardless of who is assisting, it is the homeowner's responsibility to keep all lines of communication open.

Be persistent, take initiative. It is vital that you stay in communication.

Each time you contact the servicer, note the agent's name with whom you speak, employee I.D. number and name of the department. If your case is assigned to a customer relationship manager, underwriter, or negotiator, note their contact information as well.

Asking for a loan modification

What is a loan modification? A loan modification is when a term/terms of the loan change or are modified.

For instance, if even one term is changed, it is considered a loan modification. In some cases, loan modifications will not reduce the mortgage payment.

A mortgage servicer may decide to lower your interest rate, extend the years on the loan, or add the delinquency amount towards the end of balance or a combination of 2 or 3 of these. Your mortgage company is required to follow the investors' guidelines. Keep in mind, not all borrowers have the same investor. Therefore, loan modifications will differ from each another. In some cases, the loan may have more than one investor.

Before applying for a loan modification, the first step is to have a realistic goal. Be realistic about whether the home is affordable. Is the hardship temporary or permanent?

As a housing counselor, 90 percent of my calls were homeowners asking for a loan modification. Before contacting the mortgage company, know that there is a difference between an in-house loan modification and the Making Home Affordable government modification known as HAMP.

Common Loan Modifications

1. In-house loan modification

2. Making Home Affordable government modification, known as HAMP.

Loan modifications may be short-term or long-term, and have an expiration date. Before your loan modification is granted, it is imperative to review the guidelines/terms in detail.

Short Term Modification: A short-term loan modification is a loan modification for anywhere from six months to a year.

Long-Term Modification: A long-term modification may be for anywhere from one year to the end of the term of loan.

Depending on your investors' guidelines, you may be allowed to apply at least once or multiple times throughout the term of the loan. If you have become delinquent on a loan modification, don't be afraid to ask your servicer for other options.

Common Misconceptions about the MHA Program

1. A loan modification will reduce the mortgage payment.

Fact: A loan modification may change any of the terms on the loan, such as lowering the interest rate, extending the years on the loan, or adding a delinquency amount to the end of the balance. In some cases, it may increase the mortgage payment. Every case is different. Every loan that is modified will not always reduce the mortgage payment.

2. Housing Counseling Agencies may complete my loan modification application.

Fact: Housing counseling agencies educate homeowners. They offer resources and referrals. In most cases, agencies are unable to complete your application due to liability/legal purposes.

3. Upon completion of the trial program, the HAMP Program will be awarded.

Fact: A "trial/forbearance program" will not guarantee the HAMP Program.

4. Servicers would rather foreclose on my home than grant a loan modification.

Fact: Foreclosing on a home will not only cost the borrower, but the mortgage company as well. Foreclosure fees are costly, more than $40,000 (attorney fees, court cost, etc.).

5. Modifying a loan is a quick process.

Fact: Mortgage companies established new protocols and many times hire third party agencies. Many loan modification applications are on hold or piled up. In some cases, mortgage companies are overloaded with hardship applications, are understaffed, or simply unorganized. Modifying a loan will take time.

Additional Properties

Investors are interested in knowing that the borrower is doing everything possible to save their primary home. If a borrower has additional rental/investment properties that are current, the investor will need a letter of explanation, lease agreement and proof of income. Depending on your investors' guidelines, there may be retention options for your second home.

Our Cultural Beliefs

We have our own beliefs and values. In some cultures, it is believed we need to financially support our family (mother, father, siblings). However, at some point our lives transition and our priorities may change.

Some of our culture beliefs and values may change. For example, planning a marriage, having a family, or going away for college may have an impact on the family's finances. If you no longer receive a contribution from a family member and you are struggling to pay the mortgage, review your expenses, and create a budget.

Some homeowners decide to obtain a second job, until they find an alternative way to increase their income.

However, ask yourself, "Do I need to work two jobs and/or overtime in order to afford the mortgage? And for how long?" Be realistic.

Collections Department

No doubt when we become delinquent, we receive repeated calls from the collections department. It is their protocol to collect the deficiency and bring the mortgage current. If you are being reviewed for a loan modification, ask the collections department to transfer you to the appropriate department.

If you are currently working with someone specifically or with loss mitigation, let the collections department know. Also, if you are willing to make a partial payment, ask the servicer if they are willing to accept a partial payment. If so, how will that partial payment be applied to your balance?

Hardship Documentation

Each investor has specific guidelines and require specific documentation. The following list is an example of common documents that may be requested.

1. 1040
2. Tax Extension Form 8879
3. Schedule C
4. Schedule E
5. Schedule B
6. Schedule K-1
7. Retirement Statements
8. IRS Transcripts
9. Pension Award Letter
10. Unemployment Benefits
11. Social Security Award Letter
12. Supplemental Security Income letter
13. Government savings bond
14. Leave Earnings Statement
15. Profit & Loss
16. Lease Agreement
17. Boarder - Room Rental
18. Disability Policy

19. Death Benefits statement
20. Dodd-Frank Certificate
21. Divorce Decree
22. Separation Agreement
23. Court Order (Alimony)
24. Court Order (Child Support)
25. Quit Claim Deed
26. Borrower name change
27. Non-borrower Information
28. HHF 3rd Party State Authorization
29. Power of Attorney letter
30. Hazard Insurance
31. Property Taxes
32. HOA Dues Letter
33. 1003 Application
34. Pay Stubs
35. Bank Statements
36. Hardship Letter
37. Letter of Explanation

Resubmitting Hardship Documentation

Homeowners resubmit hardship documentation constantly, sometimes more than 50 pages at once. The forms will be requested repeatedly because specific documents have to be current (within the past 30 days, 90 days or within one year) depending on your investor.

The offer letter or hardship package will have a deadline. Submit documentation before the deadline. (If there is not a deadline on the form, ask the representative).

I would not rush through documents; take the time to review all documentation in its entirety. Also, be sure to fill out all documents completely and accurately.

Quick tips to review:

- Investors require current/updated document.
- Non-profit agencies may be able to print certain documents free of charge. If you're constantly going to have to submit documents and need to do a lot of printing, I recommend investing in a fax/printer.
- Turn in all documents before the expiration date.
- Do your homework; you have deadlines.
- Make sure all boxes are checked.
- Missed checked boxes may delay the entire process.
- Complete all the sections that apply to you.
- If it applies to you as the borrower/co-borrower, fill it out, do not leave it blank.
- Signatures and dates are completed.
- Make sure all required signatures and dates are completed.
- Letters of Explanation need to be dated and signed by all borrowers.

- Letters of explanation should include specific details. I recommend including who, what, when, where, why, how much. Date and sign the document.
- Third Party Agencies, Do **NOT** pay any third party agencies who may be promising to modify your loan. There are non-profit agencies to assist and counsel you with your modification application for free.
- Use enough time to go through each form carefully. Complete each and every form that is required. Remember, forms have deadlines. Don't forget to *cross your t's and dot your i's*.
- If your circumstance has changed and you are reapplying, your financials will need to be updated and resubmitted to the servicer. It is vital that all documentation be current.
- Therefore, save all your documentation and make copies for yourself. Continue to resubmit current documentation until a final decision is made.

It may become overwhelming having to fax, mail and print documents that are required. Verify with your mortgage company if you can print and fax any of the documents at a local branch.

Other options to explore: visit a local library or a nonprofit housing counseling agency and ask about printing and faxing services.

Common Mistakes found:

Undocumented income: Have your expenses aligned. Rental income, pensions, 401k, or any large portion of cash (such as a bank account) will have to be explained to your servicer/lender by writing a letter of explanation (LOE).

Letter of explanation: Include all signatures, dates, and amounts.

Award Letter: Award letters are usually requested if you are receiving some type of government assistance, such as social security or some kind of pension.

Bank statements: Nowadays, most statements include the total number of pages. All pages should be sent to servicer, even if they are blank.

For example, let's say you receive your bank statement, totaling 15 pages. Page 14 incudes advertisements and page 15 is blank. Pages 14 and 15 should still be included with your hardship package.

Getting the Runaround

Borrowers are receiving inconsistent information, getting the run around, resubmitting documentation repeatedly. Lenders indicate, "It got misplaced or we never received it." If this happens to you, who should be responsible for this type of miscommunication?

Borrowers feel threatened and verbally mistreated by a representative, one of many reasons why borrowers avoid their phone calls. Homeowners understand the urgency to stay current, making payments on time, but yet express the following:

1. "I'm afraid to answer the call, the bank keeps calling. I'm terrified. I prefer not to open the mail."

2. "I keep getting transferred from one department to another. Customer service representatives give me different answers. I get confused with different information. I don't know whether to believe them or not."

3. "I just lost my job and don't have enough money. I spent $37 faxing the hardship documentation. Yet, the representative tells me they did not receive my documents. I can't afford to be resubmitting the documentation over and over!"

4. "I've been working on the loan modification for the past two years, and I keep getting the runaround. The mortgage company continues to say, "It's under review." I keep sending documentation over and over."

5. "The representatives don't listen. The collections department keeps asking for a payment, even after letting them know I'm working with the loss mitigation department."

Making A Complaint Against Your Mortgage Servicer

Many homeowners have mentioned they have been working on the loan modification process for the past two years. Before escalating the situation or filing a complaint, there are many steps a homeowner may take to ensure they have done their best.

Note the following steps:

1. Keep a journal: Contact your servicer on a weekly basis. Always ask the representative for their name and employee I.D. number. Notate the name and the direct contact number. If you are being transferred from one department to another, write down the information for each department.

2. Get an update on the account at least once a week. For verification purposes, representatives will want to clarify if your information is accurate. It may sound redundant

each time you call, but know that it's for security purposes. If you have been denied and there has been a change in circumstance, consider reapplying. Ask the servicer how often you may apply.

3. Sometimes we get bombarded with so much information and become frustrated, but calling and acting outraged may result in the phone call being dropped. Some representatives can only handle so much and have the right to refuse service. If you have not been able to resolve a customer service matter, politely request to speak with a supervisor or manager. You may also request that your situation be escalated.

If the situation has been escalated and you have followed the chain of command, you may contact the following agencies for additional information: The State Attorney General, Comptroller of the Currency, Administrator of National Banks, Federal Trade Commission or The Better Business Bureau.

Several homeowners who find it difficult to escalate the issue with the servicer will either contact the media, write a letter to the president, or contact their attorney, with expectations that the circumstance will be resolved. However, there is no guarantee on how long it will take to resolve a complaint. Therefore, if you go through these channels, it is imperative to continue to contact your servicer.

If you are resolving an escalation and your foreclosure is active, request the servicer to place the foreclosure process on hold until a final decision is made. Sometimes this is allowed.

Importance of Contacting the Mortgage Company

If you are receiving assistance from a housing counselor, realtor or any third party, it is imperative that you, as the borrower, keep in contact with your servicer. Your counselor or realtor are not responsible for finding out about every update or the final outcome. It is your responsibility to follow up with the mortgage company/ servicer to review your status.

Dealing with Being Denied

Your investor wants to know if you are able to afford your home. However, circumstances may change and investors may reconsider you. The following are reasons why borrowers are denied:

1. Foreclosure timeframe: Time is crucial; there may not be sufficient time to apply. Servicers have a timeframe to determine if there is enough time to apply for options or programs.

2. Income: Your investor wants to know if you can afford the home. The final

decision is based on your investor's guidelines. Every loan has different guidelines. Eligibility will be determine based on your credit, gross monthly income, debt expenses, debt to income ratio and additional factors.

3. Credit: Your investors want to determine if you have additional obligations. For example, if your investor denied you due to insufficient income based on your credit, review your credit and dispute any information impacting the investors' decision. Your investor has specific guidelines regarding your credit report.

I recommend that you dispute any information that has been paid for or information that may not belong to you. If you have set up payment arrangements with any collection agency, request for an agreement letter, so you have proof. (You have a right to review your credit report once a year for free. Visit www.annualcreditreport.com

Credit Report

In order to dispute any information on your credit report, it is recommended to write a letter to both the credit bureau and creditor. They further investigate the situation and you should receive an answer within 30 days. However, it is recommended that you do this in writing and print copies, so that you have proof.

The credit score is divided into the following five categories: History, length of credit, how much you owe (balance), type of credit accounts you have open, and credit accounts recently opened. When applying for hardship assistance, certain options/programs will require the underwriter to review all aspects of the credit report.

If you have many credit cards that you would like to combine to lower the interest rate then consider a debt management program (DMP). Debt management program agencies should be non-profit. Some agencies will provide you with free counseling. If you decide to join a DMP there may be a small fee. You should be able to receive an estimate. A DMP counselor will recommend the most effective option based on your current situation and goal. The following is a list of the common options usually prescribed after speaking to a DMP Counselor: DMP, legal advice, judgment proof, or settling directly with the creditor.

Contracts/Forms/Deadline

Before you sign any documentation, make sure you understand the agreement. If there is any unfamiliar terminology, contact your lender/loan officer to review the verbiage. Or if you are working with your local trustworthy attorney that specializes in real estate, have them explain the contract before you acknowledge the contract.

Children Affected By Foreclosures

Children may be affected psychologically by the housing industry. Children may sense if their family is going through financial strain. Foreclosure is a deadly disease. It is recommended you take the time to communicate with your children, in the event you have to transition from the home.

Foreclosure may cause a burden on children. In my experience, Ive witnessed a child realizes they are losing their home – they become scared, angry and frustrated.

If you end up having to transition from the home, communicate with your child in a positive, effective manner.

I came across the Soto family during a counseling session. The Sotos, a family of four, were impacted by Hurricane Katrina. Their interest rate reset and their mortgage payments increased. The family struggled to repair the home after the hurricane.

Fifteen year old son, Mario, noticed his parents were financially struggling and became frustrated, unable to bear the thought of losing their home. Gradually, Mario became depressed, unable to cope with his parents' financial situation.

Mrs. Soto refused to give up their home. She continued to negotiate with the mortgage company. Maria cried each night, devastated about losing her home.

Mario left his home a few days later. Maria's siblings notified her that Mario was staying with relatives in Mexico.

Maria, devastated, promised her son she would find a way to overcome the financial hardship. Eventually Maria's home was foreclosed.

After discovering the feeling of emptiness, her first priority was her family. Maria experienced the loss of her family and home.

During An Active Foreclosure

If the mortgage company indicates you're in foreclosure, and you're not sure what steps to take, here are some suggestions:

1. Consider post-foreclosure counseling (free of charge) with a HUD-approved counseling agency to familiarize yourself with the process. Contact United Way at 211 or **888.995.hope**

2. Verify the foreclosure timeline in your state. You can find foreclosure information by visiting www.foreclosurelaw.org or contacting your local HUD office.

3. Before applying for disposition options: verify if the state you reside in has a redemption period. A redemption period allows the homeowner to reacquire property lost due to a foreclosure.

4. Contact your servicer and ask to speak to the foreclosure department or seek foreclosure legal advice free of

charge.

5. Apply for assistance. Certain services may allow homeowners to apply for assistance during an active foreclosure. If you are in an active foreclosure, you want to ask the servicer if they are willing to accept your mortgage payment.

If your servicer is not accepting payments while under a review, save the mortgage payment, until a final decision is made.

6. If your servicer is reviewing you for options/programs and you have a foreclosure sale date, ask your servicer if they are going to A). Place your foreclosure on hold or B). Postpone the sale date.

7. If your servicer refers you to their attorney, gather as much information as possible and seek non-profit legal advice. There are non-profit resources that provide legal advice or assistance. Contact your local United Way by dialing 211 and asking for legal services.

Filing for Bankruptcy

It is not guaranteed that a bankruptcy will always save a home. It may buy you some time to avoid foreclosure. However, make sure there is sufficient income to continue to afford the mortgage payment. Determine if the household has sufficient time and income.

Short Sale

A Short Sale is when you sell your home for less than what you owe.

For example, you owe $200,000 but your home is valued at $100,000.

Short sales may impact your credit score. However, it is less of an impact on your credit compared to a foreclosure.

If you decide to apply for a short sale, the servicer will have to approve the short sale. The lender will have to make sure there is enough time to apply for a short sale. If the lender allows you to apply for a short sale, look for a realtor who is experienced in short sales.

The realtor will then complete the appropriate agreement/paperwork and submit it to the lender. If you have a buyer, the investor will review the offer and decide to either approve or deny.

Questions to ask the mortgage company about a Short Sale:

1. How long will the home be placed in the market?
2. Do I continue to make the mortgage payment?
3. Will you accept partial payment?
4. During a short sale, if there is a change in circumstance, may I reapply for retention options? (Loan modification, reinstatement, payment plan, and partial claim).
5. Am I currently in an active foreclosure?
6. Do I have a foreclosure sale date?
7. If circumstances change, how often may I reapply for assistance during the process of a short sale?

Several mortgage companies will allow you to reapply if your circumstance has changed financially. However, MHA Program and traditional options have specific timeframes and deadlines. Guidelines may change at any point. Therefore, contact the servicer on a weekly basis.

Getting Treated For A Nervous Breakdown

When we are experiencing a tremendous loss, where do we stand? How do we cope mentally?

Losing our homes may impact us mentally and physically.

Throughout my counseling career, homeowners have called desperately looking for assistance. Every day it was a different story of how the servicer foreclosed on their home.

Mrs. Bryan is an example of how life can change instantly.

One evening Mrs. Bryan decided to surprise Mr. Bryan at work. She walked into a nightmare of infidelity. She found Mr. Bryan with a mistress. For weeks, Mrs. Bryan tried to cope with the devastating news. She eventually decided to separate.

During their separation, Mrs. Bryan stayed at home, hoping one day they would reconcile and work things through. Mr. Bryan continued his affair, though, and Mrs. Bryan eventually filed for divorce.

Mrs. Bryan walked away penniless, moving into a mobile home. She became frustrated, unable to find employment. Her friends were no longer able to financially support her. Slowly, Mrs. Bryan's lifestyle changed.

According to Mrs. Bryan, Mr. Bryan's business failed after Hurricane Katrina in 2005 and he claimed he was unable to assist her financially. She became depressed and homeless.

Mrs. Bryan never worked in her life nor obtained an education. She was always taken care of financially, so it was difficult for her to obtain employment and be on her own.

She realized she would not be able to afford the home on her own so there was no point in trying to fight for the home in court. Eventually, the home was foreclosed.

Mrs. Bryan adopted a new lifestyle; she began to work side jobs that paid cash and sought therapy and housing counseling.

Transitioning From A Home

Most servicers recommend that a mortgage payment ought to be less than 33 percent of our total gross income. However, most times we end up paying above 33 percent. Prior to moving into a home, I recommend completing a " first time homeowner" course. A first time homeowner course provides information on how to financially manage a mortgage. Not to mention, several housing counseling agencies may award grants. Keep in mind, housing grants have specific guidelines and are based upon availability.

Make sure the educational course is free of charge. Some agencies that provide the counseling charge a small fee, while others do not. Do your research.

The first step is creating an action plan. You and your counselor will create a budget of your monthly/annual expenses.

In the event that you have to transition from the home, speak to your servicer.

They may offer transitional options or programs.

Temporary Housing

So after you lose your home, where do you go? Homeowners who have lost their homes can either rent an apartment or basement, or find a roommate. Also, visit your local church and nonprofit organizations and ask if they offer their facilities in exchange for assistance (cleaning, administration, etc.). Remember, this is a temporary situation. There is always a fresh start.

Contact your local HUD office if you need assistance with housing referrals.

We cannot imagine transitioning from our home. We work so hard to keep our homes, but there are some things that we have no control over. Remember, there is always a fresh start.

Trust, have faith and strength. There is always a first time for everything. If it is affecting your health, seek professional help. Consult a professional counselor, a local non-profit church, or family and friends. You can make a fresh start.

Struggling Homeowners

A financial transition may exhaust a homeowner and may cause them to lose hope. Homeowners become exhausted working with lenders or services trying to apply for assistance.

Homeowners continue to experience tragic episodes of foreclosure. *You are not alone, and it is important to speak to someone.* There are many non-profit agencies that provide housing counseling and educational resources. There isn't always an answer as to why some of us go though certain situations and others don't. Sometimes we tend to read too much into blogs, news and gossip. But the truth is, everyone experiences different situations with similar feelings: frustration, hurt, and manipulation.

Again, you are not alone. The following homeowners were once delinquent on their mortgages. There are many homeowners who, like you, are struggling. Some homeowners have been applying for loan modifications for the past two to three years. After hundreds of conference calls, I came across respectable representatives that have been professionally trained and educated to provide you with the respect and education you deserve.

1. Ms. Josie was placed in foreclosure after discovering she was unable to afford the loan modification. There was insufficient time to apply for a short sale. Shortly after the home was placed in a foreclosure sale, Josie was told she had 4-6 weeks to vacate the property. Josie made sure she did everything she could to redeem her home.

I recommended Ms. Josie inquire about pre-foreclosure programs, such as "Deed for Lease" or "Cash for Keys." We contacted the mortgage company. We were transferred to the servicer's attorney department. No one was available at the time. I advised Ms. Josie to look for foreclosure legal advice and review the foreclosure laws in her state.

2. Mr. Jackson was a successful businessman until his work hours slowly began to be reduced. Not only did he lose income, but he was losing his wife and about to lose his mind. He was very much in love with his wife and didn't realize his financial situation would become a burden to his family. Mr. Jackson walked into the bedroom to find Mrs. Jackson packing, planning to leave

the marriage, because she was financially stressed.

Mr. Jackson became emotionally depressed, stating all he wanted to do was "wash the pain away." Mr. Jackson prayed every night for strength and hope. Gradually, Mr. Jackson's hours increased. Fortunately, Mr. Jackson continued to work with his mortgage company and eventually qualified for a loan modification.

Once a borrower has an increase of income and there has been a change in circumstance, they should reapply for long term options/programs, such as a modification.

3. Ms. Edmond spoke to her servicer and was told her case was not under review due to missing documentation. We placed a conference call to the servicer and spoke to David. David indicated Ms. Edmond's file had been assigned to a processor and a decision would be made soon (The timeframe was not provided). David indicated that if Ms. Edmond would like to review future updates, she could view

them on their website.

Until Ms. Edmond received the final decision, she continued to receive standard letters and calls from the collections department.

The lenders and servicers follow a protocol. If the borrower is more than 30 days delinquent, the borrower will be notified by the collections department. It is imperative for the borrower to contact the servicer each week for a status update until a final decision is made.

4. Mr. Ramos indicated he was denied for a loan modification due to documentation that had not been received. According to the borrower, he was asked to submit hardship documents repeatedly. The homeowner felt he was getting the runaround with the servicer.

Before contacting the servicer, we updated the borrower's financials, and based on his monthly expenses, he demonstrated he was able to afford the mortgage payment.

Mr. Ramos and I contacted his servicer to clarify the denial. We spoke to

Rachel. Rachel indicated the borrower was denied due to them not receiving his hardship documentation on time. However, his loan was being reviewed for the second time. Rachel indicated a negotiator contacted Mr. Ramos to request the missing documentation and was unable to get ahold of Mr. Ramos. Rachel advised Mr. Ramos to fax the hardship documents they previously requested.

If you are unable to make a mortgage payment, ask your servicer if they are willing to accept partial payments. Otherwise, save any monetary amount until the servicer makes a final decision.

If you are denied for retention options, ask the servicer why you were denied. If you believe there is an error, ask to dispute the error (appeal) and request if there may be a second review, especially if there is a "change in circumstance."

5. Mrs. Roberts was two months delinquent due to funeral expenses. In addition, Mrs. Roberts' hourly wages were reduced from $20.00/hour to $18.00/hour, a deficit of $472.90 a

month and $33,000 in savings.

We created an action plan and contacted the mortgage company. The servicer recommended Mrs. Roberts apply for mortgage assistance via the Internet. After Mrs. Roberts completed the online application, she would have to contact the mortgage company on a weekly basis for a status update.

I advise homeowners that it is imperative to keep in contact with the mortgage company on a weekly basis until a final decision is made.

6. Mrs. Smith was seven months delinquent with a notice of intent to foreclose. She was declined for MHA Loan Modification. We reviewed her financials with the servicer. Based on Mrs. Smith's financials, she did not qualify for any retention options, due to the fact that that her mortgage payment was below 31% of her income. The borrower did not have any savings to pay the delinquency amount and was unable to afford a repayment plan. In order to avoid foreclosure, the servicer suggested applying for pre-foreclosure

options. However, Mrs. Smith refused and instead decided to seek legal advice.

7. Mr. Rogers was offered a trial payment from April 2012 through July 2012. Mr. Rogers indicated he received a letter with the temporary payment based on a gross income of $2,500/month. Mr. Rogers indicated the gross income was incorrect and instead was $1,700/month.

After reviewing Mr. Rogers' financials, I recommended a short sale to Mr. Rogers. He refused to sell the home and decided to appeal the decision. Mr. Rogers and I contacted the servicer and spoke to Vince. Vince indicated if the trial program is declined, there is no guarantee there will be an additional offer.

Vince advised Mr. Rogers that if he appealed the trial payment, he would need to email the underwriter to determine if the income could be corrected. He recommended Mr. Rogers make the trial payment so that the trial plan would not be canceled. The borrower agreed. In the mean time, his appeal would be reviewed.

8. Mr. Lee indicated his home was foreclosed and auctioned. He stated that he was advised five days prior to his home going into auction, which did not allow time to apply for assistance. Mr. Lee's investor was participating in a rental program. However, there was not enough time to apply for assistance due to the foreclosure timeframe.

It is imperative to acknowledge mortgage correspondence. Prepare yourself and meet those deadlines.

9. Ms. Morris was declined for a loan modification due to insufficient income (based upon investor's guidelines). We contacted her servicer to get a status update. Ms. Morris had a foreclosure sale date.

In order to reapply for assistance, she would have to wait at least 90 days. However, there would not be sufficient time to reapply because the foreclosure sale would fall before the 90-day period.

I suggested Ms. Morris seek legal advice and find out what the foreclosure laws are in her state. I referred her to **www.foreclosurelaw.org**

10. Mrs. Jacks was unemployed for six months. During her unemployment she received unemployment benefits and managed to make the mortgage payment each month.

She applied for assistance and, being that she was less than 30 days delinquent, she was denied for assistance.

Fortunately, Mrs. Jacks obtained employment and was able to increase her income. I recommended to her that during any short term hardship, she should discuss temporary options with her servicer, such as a special forbearance.

11. Mrs. Mills is five months delinquent due to unemployment. It's been three months since she last spoke to her servicer. The borrower indicated she was denied for a loan modification. Her goal was to keep her home and she had managed to increase her income.

We contacted the mortgage company for

a status update, and the servicer indicated that Mrs. Mills, at the time, was in foreclosure, without a sale date.

The servicer once again reviewed her financials. However, based on Mrs. Mills' financials, she was not eligible for a loan modification. She decided to seek legal advice.

12. Mr. Parker was denied twice from the HAMP Program due to investors' guidelines. The borrower became distraught at having to reapply and began to wonder if the mortgage servicer was in compliance with the MHA Program.

Mr. Parker questioned if the mortgage company was following the appropriate procedures. He was unsure of the servicers' protocol. I recommended Mr. Parker speak to a supervisor or manager.

13. Mr. Spring is 22 months delinquent due to loss of income. Mr. Spring is able to continue to make his mortgage payment, however he is unable to reinstate the loan and has been denied for a loan modification.

The balance is approximately $518,000 with a value of $381,000. In order to avoid foreclosure, Mr. Spring tried to reapply for a loan modification (since there has been a change of circumstance) and anticipates his home will increase in value.

14. Ms. Daniels has been working on a loan modification for the past two years. She is seeking a loan modification to lower her mortgage payment. However, the mortgage payment is less than 31% of her gross monthly income and has been denied for a loan modification.

The servicer recommended she apply for a special forbearance. However, Ms. Daniels denied the offer.

The borrower indicated the mortgage payment is not affordable at 31 % and she would have to either increase her income, or apply for a pre-foreclosure sale.

15. Mr. Knight was denied for a loan modification, after a year, due to missing documents. However, the borrower indicated he spoke to the servicer and resubmitted the missing

documentation. The servicer indicated they contacted him five times and were unable to get ahold of him.

Mr. Knight disagreed with the servicer, indicating he did not receive any voicemails or phone calls. Despite the discrepancy, he was allowed to reapply per investors' guidelines.

I recommended to Mr. Knight that anytime there is a change in circumstance, to reapply for assistance. A final decision will be based on your investor's guidelines.

Also, if faced with foreclosure, review local foreclosure laws. Continue to contact the servicer on a weekly basis for updates. To escalate any communication barriers, ask to speak to a supervisor or manager. If unable to resolve an escalated case with a manager and you feel the servicer is not taking appropriate steps, then follow the chain of command. You may also contact the Office of the Comptroller of the Currency at 1-800-613-6743.

16. Ms. Cane received an offer letter for a "Special Forbearance." She and I

contacted the servicer. We were advised the offer had expired and the borrower would have to reapply.

Ms. Cane was unsure whether to reapply for assistance or place the home for sale. She had been borrowing money to keep her mortgage current. However, if assistance was not provided, she would eventually become delinquent.

In order to avoid a foreclosure, Ms. Cane had to make a decision of either selling the home or increasing her income. Ms. Cane was encouraged to continue to contact the servicer on a weekly basis if she applies for any of the loss mitigation options.

17. Mr. Gonzalez was recently denied for a loan modification. The borrower is 33 months delinquent and on a (long term) fixed income.

The borrower is paid $300 to $400 cash a week (side job). He did not report the additional income when applying for the loan modification.

After reviewing the homeowner's budget, it was determined that there is sufficient income to continue with a mortgage payment.

Although the borrower would like to keep his home, he will have to ask the servicer if there is sufficient time to reapply for a loan modification.

18. According to Ms. Perez, she received a modification on October 2012. Ms. Perez indicated she signed the agreement, and faxed and mailed the agreement from the local branch. In March 2013, she received a foreclosure notice. The borrower contacted the servicer and was advised she needed to submit new documents. By this time, she was in a foreclosure status with no sale date. Ms. Perez felt she was getting the runaround. I advised my client to take the following steps:

a. If you have not been able to resolve the matter with a manager, escalate the matter and follow the chain of command.

b. Find out if your case under violation and if your lender is taking appropriate steps.

c. If you do not qualify for a loan modification, consider alternative loss mitigation options.

d. Consider legal advice to review foreclosure laws and housing rights as a homeowner.

e. If you are unable to resolve your case with your servicer manager and feel your servicer is not taking appropriate steps or that they are not enforcing fair and honest treatment, contact your state attorney general and the Office of the Comptroller of the Currency at 1-800-613-6743.

19. Mrs. Bishop had a foreclosure sale date for the following day and was able to extend the sale date for up to two weeks. (Mrs. Bishop's loan is a non-government loan). The borrower had surgery and is on medical leave for eight weeks. She has applied for disability, but it takes a number of weeks for disability to be processed. Her only source of income at this time is her rental income, $1400/month.

After reviewing the borrower's budget, we estimated a $2507 deficit. Based on the borrower's current financial situation, there may not be sufficient time to apply for a short sale or deed in lieu. As a result, she will seek foreclosure legal advice to find out what the foreclosure law is in her state.

20. Mr. Saenz is less than 30 days delinquent and would like a loan modification. Mr. Saenz indicates he was denied for the HAMP Program due to missing documents. The servicer informed the borrower that the missing form had been found. However, he was denied due to his investors' guidelines.

I recommended that Mr. Saenz reapply for assistance, if there has been a change in circumstance (Borrower's income and financials will be compared to the previous ones). We contacted his servicer and spoke to Sophia. Sophia suggested he apply for the HARP Program since he is current. The borrower refused and instead continued with his mortgage payment.

21. Ms. Salazar would like to keep her home. The borrower is in imminent default and has been applying for a loan

modification as of 2010. Ms. Salazar indicated one department advised her case was closed and was sent to the loss mitigation department. The borrower called the loss mitigation department and was advised the Home Preservation Department was handling her case. The Home Preservation Department then transferred her back to customer service.

The borrower continued to get the runaround. Finally, in December 2011, she was pre-approved for a trial modification. The trial modification payment was higher then her original payment (due to property taxes increasing). Ms. Salazar decided to decline the loan modification and instead sell the property.

22. Mrs. Peters indicated she verbally received a traditional loan modification with a modified mortgage payment of $1,077.04. The borrower indicated her mortgage payment increased by $10.49.

Mrs. Peters also indicated she did not receive the loan modification agreement in writing and instead was sent a foreclosure sale notice.

We contacted the servicer and spoke to Greg. Greg suggested she reapply for a MHA Loan modification. However, due to her foreclosure timeframe, there would not be enough time and will not guarantee that the borrower will qualify. Therefore, my client is taking a risk: should she appeal or reapply?

If the borrower wants to proceed with the traditional loan modification, she would have to wait to receive the documents (by mail), sign and date them, and send them back immediately in order to avoid foreclosure. Greg indicated if my client does not comply with the traditional loan modification then her other options would be to reinstate the loan or a repayment plan Mrs. Peters decided to seek legal advice and wait for a written agreement on the final loan modification.

23. Mr. Fu was approximately 30 months delinquent due to a reduction in work hours. Mr. Fu continued to experience a reduction in work hours. After reviewing Mr. Fu's budget, my client is in a $1600 deficit. The borrower indicates he has been using his

savings each month to buy his necessities. His goal is to keep his home.

Mr. Fu's savings were slowly diminishing. I recommended that Mr. Fu find ways to increase his income, otherwise consider selling the property. In the mean time, submit a completed hardship package to his servicer and seek legal advice.

24. Mrs. O'Neal indicated she was denied for the MHA HAMP Program. We updated her financials and realized she has a deficit of $626 a month. The O'Neal's indicated income would not be increasing; Mr. and Mrs. O'Neal are retired and live on a fixed income.

Based on the information, I recommended a short sale. I advised my client that there is not sufficient income, especially if her income will not increase. The client understood. I provided her with rental housing resources.

The borrower indicated two weeks later she received a hardship package from her new servicer. I advised my client to complete the package and submit it to the servicer. Once the package is submitted, stay in contact with the mortgage servicer each week until a final decision is made.

25. Mrs. Goodwin, a resident of Georgia, is hoping to qualify for the HAFA program, which may include an incentive. She can no longer afford her mortgage. I advised Mrs. Goodwin to begin researching affordable housing. I referred my client to the GA Department of Community Affairs (404) 679-4940, Midtown Assistance (404) 679-4940 & Mercy Housing (404) 873-3887.

26. Ms. Garson is in active foreclosure and refuses to sell her home. The borrower is not in agreement with the lender's offer. The lender is offering her $959/month for two-years/ interest only.

I advised Ms. Garson that if she disagrees with the lender's offer, to consider selling the home. My client refuses to sell the home and is unable to pay the delinquency amount. Because Ms. Garson is in a foreclosure state she will have to make a quick decision.

She decided to seek legal advice.

27. Mr. Coleman was advised he might be pre-eligible for a forbearance plan. Once he completed a forbearance plan, he would have to pay the entire balance that was reduced/suspended or at the time he may reapply for a loan modification. Mr. Coleman instead wants a loan modification. However, a loan modification was not offered.

I advised Mr. Coleman that if the lender is not offering a loan modification, to make a choice of forbearance, until his situation changes. In order to avoid foreclosure, I recommended a short sale. However, Mr. Coleman refuses to sell his home at this time.

28. Mr. Perez is four months delinquent due to loss of employment. During his unemployment period, Mrs. Perez contributed towards household expenses and Mr. Perez utilized his rental income. After reviewing Mr. Perez's budget, he shows a $1,077 surplus. Mr. Perez would like to bring his mortgage payment current.

His mortgage ratio is 18%. Mr. Perez's goal is to keep his home and he needs assistance to reconstruct his loan. I specifically recommended a repayment plan because at the end of the month, the client shows a large surplus. Mr. Perez indicates he is currently on a repayment plan, however he is confused about the agreement.

We contacted his mortgage company and spoke to Robert. Robert indicated, "Client is currently on a repayment plan. However, Mr. Perez is one month delinquent on the repayment plan. Therefore, the repayment plan can cancel anytime because he is not in compliance with the written agreement. In addition, Mr. Perez has a foreclosure sale date."

Since the repayment plan has not yet been cancelled, it is imperative that Mr. Perez makes his payments, as agreed, because the foreclosure sale may proceed.

29. Mrs. Hill indicated she filed a complaint against the mortgage company. She indicated she was told that once she completed the trial program she would be automatically

placed in the HAMP Program. Instead, client recently completed a trial program and was denied for HAMP and was notified to pay full delinquency or the lender would start foreclosure proceedings.

I advised my client that a "trial/forbearance program" may not always guarantee a loan modification.

Make sure you fully understand the information your servicer gives or sends you. If you have any doubts or questions, call them and ask for clarity.

Referrals

The following are references that you can find online. Some of the websites provide additional resources. Certain organizations/programs may have income limitations.

1. United Way: Dial 2-1-1 (Free of charge). Or visit website www.211.org
2. Making Home Affordable: Makinghomeaffordable.gov or call 888.995.4673
3. Know Your Options: knowyouroptions.com
4. Office of the Comptroller of the Currency: Call 1.800.613.6743
5. Foreclosure Laws: foreclosurelaw.org
6. Keep Your Home California: keepyourhomecalifornia.org or call: 888.954.5337
7. To report scams, go to icintake.serveronline.net

8. Transition Assistant Programs within your state or servicer.
9. Military One Source
800.342.9647

Budget

Create a realistic budget similar to the one on the next page.

Compare all your expenses with your total monthly income. Be realistic and provide accurate amounts. This will help you assess your financial situation and hopefully decrease unnecessary expenses.

Monthly Expenses	Amount
Light Bill	
Gas Bill	
Water Bill	
Cable/Internet Bill	
Cell Phone Bill	
Groceries	
Vehicle Payment(s)	
Vehicle Insurance	
Mortgage Payment	
HOA/Mortgage Insurance	
Lawn Service/Snow Shoveling	
Gasoline	
Car Wash	
Credit Cards	
Hair Salon/Nail Shop	
Pet Care/Pet Food	
Birthdays/Holidays	
Recreation (Movies, Dining Out)	
Cigarettes/Beer & Alcohol	
Clubs/Sports	
Magazines and Subscriptions	
Total	

Quarterly/Yearly Expenses	Amount
Oil Changes/Car Maintenance	
Vehicle Registration/Inspection	
Property Taxes	
Travel/Vacation	
Total	

These are just examples; you should change the list of expenses to match your home life and true expenses.

Glossary:

HUD - Department of Housing and Urban Development

MHA - Making Home Affordable Plan

LOAN MODIFICATION - a permanent restructuring of the mortgage where one or more of the terms of a borrower's loan are changed to provide a more affordable payment. With a loan modification, the lender may agree to do one or more of the following to reduce your monthly payment: reduce the interest rate, place the past due balance at the end of your loan, an extension of the length of the term of the loan, a different type of loan or any combination of these.

SURPLUS - an amount of something left over when requirements have been met; an excess of income after all your expenses are accounted for, including the mortgage payment

DEFICIT - the amount by which something, especially a sum of money, is too small. For example, your income is too low to pay all of your monthly expenses, including your mortgage payment.

DELINQUENCY - a failure to pay an outstanding debt

UNDERWRITER-Mortgage underwriting is the process a lender uses to determine if the risk (especially the risk that the borrower will default) of offering a mortgage loan/retention option to a particular borrower is acceptable. The Underwriter follows investor and lender guidelines to determine if you qualify for any options for your loan.

www.ingramcontent.com/pod-product-compliance
Lightning Source LLC
Chambersburg PA
CBHW051724170526
45167CB00002B/791